T0082714

FADING LIGHTS

PAUL ZEPPELIN

FADING LIGHTS

iUniverse books may be ordered through booksellers or by contacting:

iUniverse
1663 Liberty Drive
Bloomington, IN 47403
www.iuniverse.com
844-349-9409

Because of the dynamic nature of the Internet, any web addresses or links contained in this book may have changed since publication and may no longer be valid. The views expressed in this work are solely those of the author and do not necessarily reflect the views of the publisher, and the publisher hereby disclaims any responsibility for them.

Any people depicted in stock imagery provided by Getty Images are models, and such images are being used for illustrative purposes only. Certain stock imagery © Getty Images.

ISBN: 978-1-6632-2083-7 (sc)
ISBN: 978-1-6632-2084-4 (e)

Library of Congress Control Number: 2021916676

Print information available on the last page.

iUniverse rev. date: 06/04/2021

Foreword

Paul Zeppelin's words come from a wealth of experiences and passions in his life. His insights cover a variety of ideas and contain valuable lessons for his readers. His poetry has a musical flow that leads the reader into the depths of his imagination and philosophy.

Readers can find solace and calm in some of these poems; however, other challenge the reader to reconsider their own thoughts and ideas. Some poems are deep and sober, while others give a more optimistic view of life. The diversity of topics and the vast history that they cover, give the reader a broad perspective of life and its joys and sorrows.

Judith Parrish Broadbent

Contents

A Silky Breeze of Our Affair

A silky breeze of our affair
Felt like a stream of tarnished gold;
I even heard a whisper of your hair,
"Farewell, it is so dreadfully cold."

The windows of your soul,
Your eyes betrayed your pain;
You knew, we'll never meet again,
You knew, you lost the title role.

Ravening seagulls fight
Above the shallow coast
Of our tearful farewell;
We couldn't see the light,
Our paradise was lost,
Our bliss turned into Hell.

Our fanatism was never mocked,
We knew no rules in our glee;
Our love boat wasn't docked,
And drowned in the loveless sea.

Our eyes didn't foresee that pain;
We thought, we will meet again.

I Am So Weird and Odd

I am so weird and odd
I plant tomatoes
In a hanging pot;
I miss the good old order
When I didn't have to toss
My words into a PC folder.

I cannot cross the gap,
What else is really new?
It's time to wipe my sap
And soar into the blue.

My loyal bosom friend,
You find God in heaven,
Please, shake his hand,
Do me a favor, tell him:

"I'll put my life in order,
I'll make another PC folder,
Just send to me your word,
I'll become a bias preacher,
I'll become a pious teacher,
I'll cut my mother's cord,
I'll create my own world.

I Dream of a World

I dream of a world,
The world of love,
The world of healing,
Not of a risen sword.
I try to rise above
This gloomy ceiling
To hear the primal word,
To see the blinding lights...
Above the horrors of my nights,
Above the fervor of the crowds,
Above the blues of rumbling skies,
Above the leaded thunderclouds
Above the daily convoluted lies.

I'll wipe the last teardrop,
The angels of my sky
Will bring the spring,
The wars will stop,
The mothers will not cry,
The birds will sing.

I dream of a world
Majestic and serene
I trust only the dead
Have never seen
The happy end...

I think I heard the word.

It Was Milano

I was alone; the bait was thrown,
The sun wastefully lit my home,
She came, the drapes were drawn,
I didn't care where she was from.

It was Milano - the capital of fashion,
The greatest cure of my depression,
With blissful vastness of the Duomo,
With grandeur of La Scala and Castello,
The awesome splendor of Lake Como,
Da Vinci's saints and not a single halo.

Her cheeks were brightly blushed,
I led her through the open door,
We kissed hello; I wanted more,
But didn't want to seem too rushed.

The blues of drowned stars
Found a harbor in her eyes,
Her skirt with ironed pleats
Guarded her luscious treats,
Only protecting window bars
Cut fiery sunset in the skies.

She sidled from her dress
Into a self-indulging joy,
The burden of a daily stress
Was guiding our set free ploy.

She was too beautiful to bear,
She was too naughty to resist,
It was a short red-hot affair
Before an altar and a priest.

Life started from a chunk of clay,
Under the unforgiving skies,
The air was cold and drenched,
The novice sun was on its way,
We waved our tearful goodbyes…
Two sinners were estranged.

Misers

They live like misers to die rich,
There is no change; there is no switch;
But God forgives, it is His trade,
Though none of the seven is obeyed.

The most high-minded of human race
Would not endorse this meek malaise,
They live like virgins never kissed,
That can't imagen what they missed.

There is enough of all they need,
But not enough to feed their greed,
The scrooge's avarice is their delight,
I bet they count money day and night.

I beg, "Please, leave your pigeonholes,
You are completely blind like moles,
Leave your lackluster filthy burrows,
And have a life, there are tomorrows."

My Bliss Is In The Making

Life isn't the cards you've got,
Life is about playing them well,
Life is
To travel, love and drink a lot,
Life is
To eat raw oysters on the shell.

I hear the loud thunder stutters,
I am on my horse; he judders
Like every self-admiring stud,
Dipping his hoofs into the mud.

A rooster of the morning after
Croaked that the time is right
For a coffee, cough and laughter
And wake the hazy country sight.

My horse runs into the stables,
Anticipating a great meal,
I drink only the reputable labels
Life is so pleasingly surreal.

I'll shave and take a shower,
I'll have my eggs and bacon,
I'll start my daily happy hour,
My bliss is in the making.

Regrets Will Miss The Aim

I walk across a shadow
Cast by a working girl;
There is a glossy void
In her inviting eyes;
A life destroyed?
A pleasure in disguise?

The sheep may die,
The fleas will jump away;
I still reluctantly comply
With rules of Judgement day.

I loathe sunsets,
Those humorless accountants
Of my sincere emotions;
They lure me like coquettes,
Beyond the looming mountains
Of my eternal pointless devotions.

Why do they bring the nights?
Why do they have to torture me?
Why don't they stop my fights?
Why don't they set me free?

The gods created us imperfect:
Regrets will miss the aim,
They never pierce the overcast,
Life is a predetermined game,
No one can change the past,
The referee won't change a verdict.

Royal Flush

The graveyards of tomorrows
Invite the doubtful and sick;
The boneyards of my sorrows
Let our lives' clocks tick.

We sailed after we met
Over a turbulent accord,
Without ever getting wet,
Without going overboard.

You were an actress,
Orgasms were faked,
I chilled the mattress,
You were already baked.

I clearly knew the prize:
We left our burrows,
We wiped our teary eyes,
Tears only dug the furrows.

You cut the deck of cards,
I dealt the suit of hearts,
You've got a Royal Flush,
It's yours to win or crush.

One mouse gets the cheese,
There were two hungry mice;
Don't guess, don't ever tease,
Enjoy the truth and pay the price.

Some Hover in the Blue

We miss the logs
In our eyes,
We see the twigs
In theirs;
We are the watchdogs
Of their lies,
Of their intrigues,
Of their affairs.

Some flew then fell,
Some fell then flew,
Some gone to hell,
Some hover in the blue.

A paper roll
Won't stop the flood,
The arms control
Won't stop the blood,
The paper cuts won't kill
The foes we have to fight,
Only the bullets will
Give them the dust to bite.

My young brave friend
Has reached his bitter end,
A short obituary of a boy,
He was only nineteen,
Another victim of a ploy,
Of a malevolent doctrine.

Spring Fiddles

Pine needles,
Thorny scent,
Spring fiddles,
Winter went.

The headless necks,
The stumps of trees,
The victims of an ax,
The soldiers at ease.

The early yellow flowers
Poke through the snow,
A very few warm hours
And streams will flow.

New spring, new strife,
The first warm breeze
Brings death and life,
Brings war and peace.

Old winter hits the skids,
Her frigid reign is over:
I placed my hefty bids
On a four-petaled clover.

They hardly ever grow,
But if you will find only one,
After this superb home run,
Your halo will forever glow.

Start Drinking

Complexity of structure,
Dark berries' rupture,
The supple aromatics
Appear quite busy;
Linguistic acrobatics
Make even me too dizzy.

A scent of apples is too crude,
The ripen cherries briefly pose;
Some hints of caramel and fruit,
A trace of daises on the nose.

Vanilla of the old-time barrels,
Wild flowers, banana peels,
The calm of Christmas carols
Nice labels, regional appeals.

The lime strikes as a mallet,
Sugary legs, lingering spices
Barely affect somebody's pallet,
But naturally elevate the prices.

The terroir and midday winds,
Acidity of tannins on the gums,
The ends of a few famous bins,
Dark chocolate and winter mums.

Hey, connoisseurs of wine,
Stop talking like doorknobs,
You are not friends of mine,
Start drinking, stupid snobs.

Straight as Rain

The moon still gleams,
I am relaxed and doze,
I lead my hazy dreams
From poetry to prose.

My tired good old train
Complains and sighs,
But I am straight as rain,
I crave much kinder skies.

I am entrenched on Earth,
A cozy cradle of my birth
With flowers and berries,
With mountains and fields,
With rivers and the ferries,
Amid the stops and yields.

I need someone to kiss,
I am requested into bliss.

A Sunset Will Fade

A red sunset inevitably fades
Like a bullfighter's rag,
And yet I will unfurl from shades,
The Southern rebels' tattered flag.

The iron horse moves us ahead,
Some never get their silver spoon,
Some never get their daily bread,
Some get too much and swoon.

I am getting used to life
Along the slowest lane,
I lost my home and wife,
She let me keep my brain.

One sparrow doesn't make a spring,
One vendor doesn't make a fair,
Although, even the mute will sing,
When life is awfully hard to bear.

Life brings me up to speed,
It offers gluttony and greed,
My aspirations will not drain,
I will not lose my pride in pain.

When facts get squeezed
Before my staggered eyes,
Life interrupts with a striptease,
I have to watch its barefaced lies.

Survival of the Fittest

Two daughters of old maven Lot?
The tale of Sodom and Gomorra says a lot;
Three daughters of King Lear?
The sadness of the story wouldn't disappear;
My daughters Katherine and Victoria?
Some love and joy, but mostly, just euphoria;
The daughters of our Revolution?
They made a deeply cherished contribution;
The sons and daughters of our Evolution?
They tried but badly missed the resolution;
Aged Charlie Darwin outlined a great solution:
A logical godsent survival of the fittest,
Just run and try to be the quickest…

The Eve of a New Year

Some crawl, the others fly;
Life-teacher is quite stern,
I study history and learn
To eat and have the pie.

Gods have their way,
They like the thrifty,
Those who just take
But never give away.
Only the fallen angel
Unwillingly stays guilty.

Confessions fell into the dust
Like teardrops of strong men;
I earned my Liberator's trust,
He left; I didn't notice when.

Euphoria and trepidation:
The eve of a New Year,
Farewell to what was dear,
I am in the midst of cheers;
But try to leave this jubilation
To close my eyes,
To calm my sighs,
To hide my tears.

The Falling Petals

A rhythmic rap
Bombards my head,
This cacophonic crap
Turns city streetlights red.

I scrutinize my previous delusions
Disguised in ornamented fabrics,
And come with joyful conclusions
About hooligans and mavericks.

The falling petals of red roses
Cover my footprints on the trails;
My pain, after the doorway closes,
Erases memories of trivial details.

My days and nights are passing by,
The lifelong train about to derail,
And I will have to say goodbye
To every innocent old fairytale.

The Fault is Mine Alone

We fought, we cried,
Our love came to an end,
The longest farewell night,
I fell apart, you didn't bend.

Our lives are squares of chessboards,
The prison cells for queens and kings,
The knights kill pieces with the swords,
The bishops skillfully pull the strings.

Life is a stage, life is a theatre,
We are acting in a blinding light,
A victory is sweet, defeat is bitter,
Like hurricanes after a quiet night.

I cannot outwit the Lord,
The fault is mine alone,
The only argument I can afford,
A loser shouldn't cast a stone.

The Foxholes of the Wars

The foxholes of the wars
Make brothers
From the strangers.
Far on the foreign shores
We fight the others,
Under the slothful angels.

We knew our useless saints,
We didn't count our sinners,
Blood runs in our veins
From the numb hearts
Of the collapsed and winners.

We're hardly proud of the past,
The relics were not hoarded;
At times, we were rewarded
Under the gloomy overcast.

They locked the exit door
Then framed us as the arts,
And sent us to fight this war
Without souls and hearts.

The ironed uniforms of heroes
Send our egos to the stars,
Only the smoky, dusty mirrors
Hid our wounds and scars.

The Loveless Hell

The gold of maples,
The blues of our skies
Ascended on my mind;
The ploys and fables,
The bitterness of lies
Was never left behind.

Our friends have gone,
Only their photos last
To face another dawn.
We lived in our past,
It was not good enough
To save our fragile love.

The pain of our farewell
Was carried in the bags;
The burning heat of hell
Morphed riches into rags.

Two self-complacent swans
Saw only black and white,
Enjoyed the early dawns,
But didn't see the daily light.

Sad loneliness and grief
Paved our pathetic path
Toward the loveless Hell;
Forgotten glee of our days,
Wasted on pessimistic plays,
Discovered a freshwater well.

The rite of spring
Was eagerly awaited;
The birds began to sing;
Love was rejuvenated.

The Madness of a Solstice

The madness of a solstice,
The murky sun is farthest
Or nearest to our equator.
Bad weather and all of this
Inviting malice to my quest
To get a break sooner or later.

Life is a bow-legged hooker,
I dwell between her legs,
I try to be a forward-looker,
I buy my joy, she only begs.

I laughed to irritate the Hell,
I cried to irritate a Holy bliss,
Life did not treat me well,
I earned my rest in peace.

I see my fortune's-tired eyes,
Mirroring pain of futile hopes,
The fallen angel in disguise
Wants me to walk tightropes.
He pulls and splits my hair,
Whipsaws my mind in half;
I only hope he wouldn't dare
To dig my grave and laugh.

Axiomatic good is still alive,
Sufficient and necessary,
It's worthy of a bloody strife
For I am believing in a fairy.

Fire-breathing dragons rattle,
My soul and body set ablaze,
It is a great Apocalyptic battle,
And seems like the end of days.

The Mermaids' Village

The Mermaids' village
By daring Paul Delvaux,
Display of a covert dream.
Divinity of every cleavage
Absorbs my feelings' flow,
And eyes reflect my gleam.

Their hearts were looted
Throughout tries-and-errors,
And only a hopeless cupid
Sending his aimless arrows.

Art lovers vigorously cast
The shades of silhouettes
On tatty tapestries of times;
The future's gloomy past
Embezzles our fruitless debts
To punishments and crimes.

I walk, I run, and crawl,
I am navigating doubts,
Avoiding my beliefs.
I try to break the wall
Between what-now's
And what-ifs.

Don't try to wake me up,
I am not completely burned,
I am in hell or paradise;
The Father passed that cup;
The fallen angel threw the dice,
And wasted everything I earned:
The silent magic of that village,
And poetry of every cleavage.

The Milk is Spilled

The milk is spilled,
It is too late to cry,
And bleach our guilt
Under the rainy sky.

A visit to a judge was brief,
The final word is still afloat,
It is our love's autumn leaf,
It is our love's sinking boat.

We couldn't reach a truce,
And totally mad and starved,
We killed the golden goose;
Poor bird is fried and carved.

We drag a heavy bag
Of our murky dreams,
And even a faded tag
Is void or so it seems.

We walk,
The wintry air gets colder,
We talk,
A furry river of your mink
Runs from your shoulder,
Streams down a full length.

The well of love is dry,
We check it every day;
Life teaches us to cry,
But doesn't teach to pray.

The Next Spring's Lovers

I wander through my doubts,
I run away from the well-known,
Across the labyrinths of crowds;
I seek a gateway to the unknown.

I hear the voices of my universe,
And loan its fables to my verse,
I walk across mosaics of the arts,
A haven for the shattered hearts.

I write; my life poetically unfurls,
Pure like an innocence of pearls;
A narrow path of my artistic walk
A bridge my critics dream to burn;
I want to fly like a red-tailed hawk,
The hardest skills I have to learn.

At times, I swim against a current,
A real honor; war helped to earn it;
I scrambled arches of rainbows,
My pardon drowned in their flows;
No guilt, no praise, no flowers,
Only a naughty hawk still hovers;
There is no one to take the blame.
We may become the next spring lovers,
Our love is burned in our passion flame.

The One Who Lived in Paris

We write because we are too lonely,
And share the misery of this disease,
But we are lonely because we write,
Nobody wants to live with those
Who only preach or fight.
And we appreciate all those,
Who understood
That our poetry is our striptease;
They simply checked under the hood.
.
"If you are lucky enough
To have lived in Paris as a young man,
Then wherever you go for the rest of your life,
It stays with you…"
I lived in Paris in my youth,
And Hemingway was right; he wrote the truth.

I never felt too lonely
Around the eternal River Seine;
Her waters always talked to me;
They knew I was the one and only,
Who wrote about Paris now and then,
Who many years ago took a knee,
And whispered to the city, soyons amis.

This verse runs faster than my typing fingers,
My memory still lingers in the war disaster;

I am in Paris in a rented pied-a-terre
Under the greatest nom de guerre
Ernest Hemingway.
Don't judge. Just for a day.

The Pain of a Reward

I am a pointer,
I am a hound,
I am a retriever,
I am verses bound.

My Pegasus, my muse, my horse
Fell from the poetic blinding sky;
A lady humbly stood nearby
Who kindly said: "I am a nurse,
I am the local dentist's help;
Don't worry, horses always yelp;
As long as she can breathe,
I'll gladly pull a few worn-out teeth."

That wasn't worth
The pain of a reward,
Whether in Heaven or on Earth,
A horse won't fall on her own sword.

She had two wings,
She bravely liked to fly
Through the fiery rings;
She kept gunpowder dry.

It is the most horrific curse:
My neck is in the noose;
My poor winged horse,
My generously gifted muse,
My inspiration for each verse,
Will never help me with the blues.

My Pegasus, my beloved horse
Fell from the psychogenic bliss;
Her lucky day; a dentist's nurse
Reserved a place to rest in peace.

The Poets Can't Imagine

What is the world without wars?
Why do we trust those very few
Who never look under the hoods?
I wonder if they ever left the woods.
Even a muse who writes my verse
Even my Pegasus, a literary horse,
Can outsmart the churches' whores,
But won't believe in something new.

My cagy brain recalls
How peace has begun:
The fires across Saigon,
The bullet-ridden walls,
They march ahead; we run;
So long. Those days have gone.

I healed my gloom,
I bit the silver bullet,
I left that cozy womb,
I had the will to do it.

Even the poets can't imagine
When our mental illness ends,
Freud is no more an engine
That runs the modern trends.

I am running my own track,
Don't ask where I am from;
I want to go back,
I want to go home.

The Road to Damascus

I am in Belle Meade's Starbucks,
A waterhole in Nashville's desert,
Oasis in a concrete labyrinth of time,
Where quiet loners lined like ducks,
Subconsciously attempting to divert
Their timid dullness into a bit sublime.

I watch their game,
While peeping at the youths,
Who try to understand and frame
Old paradigms into the newer truths.

The road to Damascus
Was never walked by me;
Only St. Paul and other rascals
Told me to fight and die or flee.
I met my rivals face to face
Just as a part of the human race.
I even shaved my thick-necked head
Like all these cocky bodyguards,
The good old boys never breastfed,
That whistle Dixie past graveyards.

The fortress of my independence
Is undeniably and quickly crumbling,
While I am futilely yet deftly mumbling
For a few timid sleepers in attendance
That there is a place for every whore,
Amid our lawmakers and gatekeepers;
I cannot coexist a minute more
With these lackluster dreary weepers,
With these dejected mourners

Daydreaming of a paradise,
But shrewdly cutting corners
Like hockey players on the ice.

There is no pulse in darkness,
Forever cold, forever heartless.
I march the road to Damascus
Under a star-studded nightly quilt,
Along a self-inflicted endless guilt.

The Stars are Few

You put a stick
In my life's spoke,
But I am a fiery wick,
I am not a shaky smoke.

The stars are few,
Above the trees,
There is no light;
I will not let you chew
A bigger piece
Than you can bite.

I watch your fancy moves
Across my tender soul,
I watch your dirty hooves
Completely out of control.

Today, I am a fallen leaf,
A past is just a past,
I live, and I won't grieve
As long as my days last.

Yet, not a single guest
Dwells in my heart,
Today, it is an empty nest
But not for your conniving art.

The Sacred Key

My Lord, I sinned:
You put the wind
Into my eager sail,
I ran away from jail.

A bad tattoo on my forearm,
A footprint of my sorrows,
A stigma of the harm,
Will follow my tomorrows.

The power of my rage
Can climb the tallest pole,
But cannot leave the cage
Hosting my tortured soul.

Below the clouds of my visions,
Among the orbits of my worlds,
I draw the lines, I make decisions,
I carve the finest filigree of words.

Look at my daring art,
Enjoy my last creation,
It is the beating heart
Of my imagination.

The midst of night,
The birds don't sing.
It is my final flight,
It is my final spring.

I turn the sacred key,
Open the golden cage,
And let my verses flee
Toward the final page.

The Sailors' Wings

The sinking submarine
In our useless periscope,
The sailors without a sin
Perishing without a hope.

The bloody sun will rise,
The fears will disappear,
I cross the trembling pier,
And hear their dire cries.

Their images are fading
In sunset's burning treat;
I walk along their sighs
Beneath my weary feet;
Their paradise is waiting
For my choked goodbyes.

The angels solved the riddle,
The sailors grew the wings,
I played the grieving strings
Of my brokenhearted fiddle.

The Sun Delays its Rounds

The tablecloth of clouds
Slid down from the skies,
The sun delays its rounds
Above our tears and cries.

The history exhumes
Our tarnished times
From our dormant tombs;
The final judgment looms
Above unwritten rhymes
Still in the fertile wombs.

Times hastily paused
The flights of jolly angels,
The gates are closed
For all prosaic strangers.

Winds swirl between
The snow-white birches,
Showing a postcard scene
With our steepled churches.

Bright as a burning match,
Crisp as a godsent sound,
Beyond my humble batch
A rainbow taps the ground.

The sun loudly wheeled
Into my silent room;
The winter's life is sealed,
The spring must bloom.

The Sun Swam in its Glee

It's all refined
Until it isn't,
Last night, I dined,
At dusk, I've risen.
I walked across
The sea of Galilee,
Barefoot, no sandals,
The sun shined in its glee,
But Judas lit the candles.

I didn't slash the knots,
I didn't share my thoughts,
I kept them under lock and key,
I was afraid of them,
I couldn't set them free,
They were too radical and bold:
"Find the innocence of lamb,
Don't sacrifice it, love and hold."

Just mark my word,
I wrote it once,
But used it many:
"Don't beg the Lord,
Just hire pros and cons,
And never pinch a penny."

I didn't unearth my birth certificate
To verify my name, address and age,
I didn't trace the first-born etiquette
Of entertaining tragedies backstage.

Today, I am reliving yesterdays,
And looking for much better plays,
Digesting morbid memories, I kept.
Tomorrows have already wept
About comedies of grievances and fears,
Over a bitter end of innocence and tears.

The Train Named Life

I travel on the train named life,
Fast, sharp and shiny as a knife,
My window seat is warm and light,
A comfortable ticket is my birthright.

I see the rivers and the clouds drift,
I owe a lot for such a priceless gift:
My family and all my loyal friends
Are vivid colors, not the blends.

"Today is yesterday's tomorrow.
Strike stubborn iron while it is hot.
Don't plan ahead on your death row.
The petals tell if we are loved or not".

We pull these revelations
From a cuff,
They help to beat our daily
Rough and tough,
These axioms and slogans
Soar over us,
Yet our trusted motto is
"In Vino Veritas!"

I almost missed the train named life,
My ticket vanished in a drunken strife,
I tried to camouflage my murky losses,
I gulped my vodka from the fire hoses.

I watch perpetual funerals of prophets
Poor guys are falling off the cliff,
Presiding over evasive wisdoms
Residing within my constant grief.

The price I pay for my enchanting life
Is more than turning on a dime:
A worthy man must have a gift
Of being wise in time.

The Winds of Change

The night has gone,
Pushed by a gentle ebb,
A beam of sunny dawn
Caught in a spider web.
I've seen this movie
Many times,
I wasted sundry words
And rhymes.

A trembling silver bell
Rings from the neck
Of my mad cow,
Oh, what the heck,
I need milk my frau.
I probably will lose
This fruitless bout:
Champagne and caviar
Gave her an agony of gout.

Kilimanjaro lost its snow,
The tundra melts its ice,
The winds of change
Already blow,
My trap is waiting
For some other mice,
El Niño tries to change
The world,
War-banners are unfurled.
Some mumble,
"Change is in the air,"
I shyly stumble,
I wouldn't dare,
I am not set to march
Under the Triumph arch.

The Wine of Hope
The Wolves Are Fed
The Word Birthed Our World
They Will Not Whisper Verses
This is My Prayer
Time walks the thinnest ice
To B.
To Beth
Too Early
Triumphant Nike
Two Autumn Leaves Fell on my Shoulders
Two Clouds Argue in the Lake

Two Feisty Noisy Ravens
Two Lonesome Stars
Two Lonesome Stars

A single napkin
For two eaters,
A second captain
On a sinking ship,
Two eager hitters
Can't share a grip.

Disaster of the smart,
Unification fell apart,
Two yet unwilling hearts
Missed by the cupid's darts.

The Wine of Hope

Don't arch your lips,
Don't ever sigh,
Don't rock your hips,
Just say goodbye.

I carved my anxious days
Among red-blooded friends,
From self-mystifying maze,
From war that never ends.

Like a god Zeus above the clouds,
I held the lightning in my hand,
I vowed, I'll refuse to trail the crowds,
I'll stop the fighting while I'm ahead.

I heard a loud thunder,
A messenger of change;
I knew I've had enough,
It was the end a lifelong slope;
It was a sweet revenge,
It was a win and not a blunder
At last, I didn't have to bluff,
I managed to embrace my hope.

I found a parking for my car,
The joint was quite dark but slick,
My friends were sitting at the bar,
And looked lie parrots on the stick.

A startling rainfall whipping
My lifelong slope;
Yet I am still sipping
The sparkling wine of hope.

The Winter Desperately Sighed

The winter desperately sighed,
And blew away the candle's flame;
It is so dark and cold; I justly tried
To solve the puzzle in this game.

The game of love,
The game of hate,
I play again and bluff
It is our second date.

I hate the vicious strife,
The lawyers and the court,
I love my seamless life,
Quite long yet awfully short.

Why do I start the game?
I wrote and lived this myth.
Why do I spark the flame?
In fear I clenched my teeth.

Listen to me, good fellow,
I am too old and stupid,
I am like a broken arrow
Aimed by a blinded cupid.

Under that cupid's spell
My rosy expectations fade;
I only hope our farewell
Won't be an egotistical parade.

The winter desperately sighed
And blew away the candle's flame,
It is so dark and cold; I justly tried
To solve the puzzle in this game.

The Wisemen Cried

We listen to the peers,
The same ole' song,
And live without fears,
Our nights are long.

The wisemen cried,
They knew tomorrows;
Our predecessors lied,
We reap the sorrows.

The willful ignorance
Of their evangelic word
Leaved toxic resonance
Of silence to the world.

Among the tombstones
With lackluster names,
Nobody ever mourns
Our religious games.

Old graves; no guards,
No thieves, no bards.

The Wolves Are Fed

At times, we kill to feel
That we are still alive;
Death is a final meal
Of one who lost his hive.

I tossed my fortune's dice:
A fork in the bumpy road
Led us to a spoon in bed;
It was a promised paradise:
The paltry sheep are saved,
And all the wolves are fed.

I am a wolf in sheep's clothing,
I am escaping hunters' loathing
Beyond a ribbon of a choppy river
Which runs into the ocean agitated;
Meanwhile, the sun hot and frustrated,
Sways kindly like a thoughtful caregiver.

I tried to save my lump-filled soul,
I failed; I didn't reach my baffled goal.
I often was the worst; rarely, the best;
My tombstone says, he has some rest.

The Word Birthed Our World

The word that birthed our hazy world
Perpetuity invites our desire to learn,
Ignites our imagination and creativity,
Then fuels our science and the arts.

Countless artists enlighten obscurity,
Our times endure the pains of elation;
An artist has to be slapped to create
As a newborn who's spanked to cry.

The arts become exuberant miracles
Overpowering the swamps of apathy,
Demoralizing the towers of antipathy,
Streaming into the hearts of humans,
Entering unnourished, craving souls,
Then turning into the waterfalls of joy,
Running into the ocean of knowledge.

Our knowledge brings creative doubts,
These doubts discover the new worlds,
Those worlds already heard the word.

There is No Emptiness

There is no emptiness
Between my lines,
I truly hate small talk,
There is no empty nest
On olden oaks and pines,
Hiding from a red-tailed hawk.

The fish hide in the shade
Close to the grassy banks,
When my good fortunes fade
The nature gives me thanks.

I fish along a shallow brook,
I catch as much as I can eat,
I let small babies off the hook,
I hope their mothers like my wit.

The stream is full of fish,
The weeping willows sway,
I have a single secret wish,
I hope my brook won't dry away.

The moon will shine and rock
Along the nights on quiet waves,
My boat will rub the creaky dock,
And wait for the sunset's blaze.

I hate the horns of crescents
On ugly helmets of the goons;
I cherish the monthly presents
Of the most generous full moons

There is No Pain in Death

There is no pain in death,
Just glory of a final breath;
I buried yet another love,
I am excited, I am free,
And still am dreaming of
The state of endless glee.

I spread my wings and fly
I hear Ravel and Debussy,
My rainbows in the sky,
My beacons in the sea.

I hear Rachmaninoff
Devouring but romantic;
He flies a long way off,
So vulnerable and frantic,
So fragile, so refined:
A sumptuous silver toll,
Nirvana for my mind,
A panacea for my soul.

The sweetest elixir of love
Descending from above,
There is no pain in death,
Just glory of a final breath.

There is Nothing Left at All

For me there is nothing left at all,
Only your shadow on the wall,
And hazy echoes of our delights
Brighten my endless daily nights.

Life is a desert, since you are gone,
Our well of joy is dreadfully dry,
It is too cold, even the mighty sun
Can't kiss and hug me from the sky.

I spoke to wisemen of this world
To blankness under their dusty wigs;
These futile leeches clung to our Lord
With their Machiavellian intrigues.

They never felt the glee I knew,
Those rooms are for the chosen few.
Forget their mighty wealth and fame,
Death is the end of our lifelong game.

From depth into the sunlit height
The church's steeple pierced the light,
The preachers talked to me in vain,
The light of love won't soothe my pain.

Tell me, a six-winged Seraphim,
Are you my guiding armless angel?
You pass above; you are so grim
As if you are a homeless stranger.

They Changed the World

Picasso and George Braque
Investigated arts of yesterday,
Made-up the analytical cubism,
Raked realism and tossed away.

Breton, Magritte, Apollinaire
Subconsciously split the hair,
And didn't care fair or unfair,
But slayed so-called "plein air".

Rousseau was childishly naive,
Matisse became a beast-fauvist,
Gauguin went through that sieve,
And poor Van Gogh was on that list.

Dali lured Gala from Paul Eluard
Then moved too quickly and too far;
Marcel Duchamp and Gino Severini
Were crazier than even Paganini.

While Gustav Klimt with his Deco
Enjoyed a high demand as Chirico,
Kandinsky started his abstraction,
Munch screamed at every function.

Smart Stieglitz quietly progressed
Chagall, Malevich and Brancusi,
Yet Georgia O'Keefe confessed
Their gallery was losing,
Le Corbusier built such a house,
That Modigliani lost his spouse.

Even Gabo, Leger and Boccioni
Once were accused of being phony,
De Kooning, Pollock, Henry Moore
Declared and won the values war.

Our Lord said, "Just mark my word,
I didn't create your modern world."

They Hump the War

We play
This torturous charade
Of our daily tragic theatre;
Our sway
Reflected in a dusty mirror
As stars and stripes parade;
We pray
A little sweet, a little bitter
And wish a victory is nearer.

Another try,
Another night,
Our mothers cry,
Our brothers fight.

We love these naughty kids,
They kill, we place the bids,
They hump the bloody war
As if it is a well-paid whore,
As if it is a seminary dorm
Right in the center of a storm;
But then they fight and roar,
Long live the army uniform.

We are still learning to forget,
We are still learning to forgive,
Our wings don't grow yet,
We are just humans,
We just grieve.

We are in our unending fall,
We are in our eternal flight,
We soar above the doubt's wall
With hope the sea of anger dried.

They Print my Shaggy Face

They print my shaggy face
On the "Most Wanted"
Posters,
I am in a hell-raising race,
I ride the scorching human
Roller-coasters.

I am waiting for arraignment
In the lawless nightly court
On charges of engagement
With a life I can't afford:
My day has no tomorrow,
I cannot pay, but borrow,
I love, eat, drink and write,
I meet a friend; I pick a fight.

I am completely guiltless
Of the insufferable crime,
But I am harshly punished:
My thoughts are wingless,
My verses have no rhyme,
My innovations vanished.

I lose from time to time,
That is my only crime,
I want to clip my wings,
I bought two wedding rings.

They Tore our Dog Tags

They see the smokes
But never see the fires,
They wear the cloaks
To camouflage desires.

At times, the truth
Unmasks their lies;
Our wasted youth
Repeats its whys.

We treasure winners,
Amass the dusty files,
We are the sinners
Caressing costly lies.

We pray at night,
We say our goodbye
And then we fight
Some live, some die.

No donuts on the tray,
No coffee in the pot,
We often curse and pray,
We play the hand we got.

We kept our words,
We bravely fought,
We earned awards;
They only sought
To reap our dog tags
And fold the flags.

They Will Not Whisper Verses

First laughing days of spring,
A glass of great champagne,
We kiss, we smile, we sing,
Forgetting our agonizing pain.

You were an island
In the sea of life,
You were a garland
I was a falling knife;
You were evasive
As a fragile dream,
I was aggressive
As a laser beam.

I would declare my wars,
You'd never pick a fight,
Sheer ecstasy of our affair
Fills our haven to its shores,
Our bodies wrapped in light,
Our souls stripped bare.

The tired spring passed by,
The summer said goodbye,
The autumn came and went,
The icy winter left its scent,
Another sunny rite of spring,
But none of us would sing.

The end of spring in our life,
We are worn-out horses,
New seasons won't arrive,
They will not visit our nook,
They will not whisper verses
To empty pages of our book.
They Will Not Whisper Verses

They'll Never Grow Old

The drums and winds of war
Fanned our vanity and pride,
Our wisdom slammed the door,
Our sobriety and reasons died.

Another graveyard wreath
Is decorated to be laid,
The messengers of death
Don't know that we prayed.

The bitter pattern we abide,
The vices aren't far behind,
The virtues are well hidden
Under that tree of Eden.

I watched the widows' veils,
I listened to the mothers' wails,
"Taps" played by brassy horns,
I wore the wreath of thorns.

Without glory, without cheers,
Some finished up stone cold,
They ended golden years,
They'll never grow old...

Eternal sadness of farewell,
Will live in my tormented soul,
I welcomed warriors to dwell,
I hung their photos on the wall.

When men are young or proud,
Too bitter are the tears of war,
Only six feet under the ground,
Their souls will leave and soar.

The winds of war
Awake our best,
Our mothers bore
The greatest heroes,
Today, they rest
Under the weeping willows.

Thirsty Lips

Survived eternity of freeze,
Burned with infinity of heat,
I won a lot, but lost too much,
I crave the Midas touch.

The wrinkles on my face
Carved with your knife
As footprints of my days,
I love my troubled life.

I am the captain of a ship,
It's time to say farewell,
The seagulls sadly weep
They think we'll sail to hell.

The moon already sleeps,
The stars forgot to shine,
I dream of thirsty lips
Sweeter than any wine.

We sail across the night,
Over the labyrinth of living,
We follow our guiding light
Toward the edge of being.

This is My Prayer

This is my prayer,
This is my last desire,
I paid the heinous fare,
I am still glowing in the fire.

My brain remembers
Those pains and screams,
Those torture chambers,
Those suicidal dreams.

The endless hallways,
Eternity of miserable days,
No hope, no faith, no love;
Life wears no velvet glove.

I saw the burning grounds,
I couldn't see the sunny sky;
Somebody from the clouds
Brings wings and lets me fly.

I had no colors in my pain,
No rainbows past the rain;
I crawled, I ran and soared,
I screamed, nobody heard.

The saints are flying in the skies
Visible to millions of eager eyes;
They pass, I hear a vain fairwell
But I am still here, in hell…

Time Doesn't Heal

Time doesn't heal,
Hearts don't forget,
It is my closing meal,
Their minds are set.

A beam of trembling light,
Not worth the candle,
We are polite and bright,
A truce before a scandal.

Fire died in water,
Love died in vain,
It was a quiet slaughter
Of our self-inflicted pain.

I rake forsaken weeds
Into another deadly sin,
I try to plant new seeds,
So easy out; so hard in.

It's easier to blow your own horn,
Than wear what has been worn,
Our bodies slowly die, we mourn,
A sinless life was not yet born…

Time Walks the Thinnest Ice

My victories were never winged,
The hymns were never sung,
My failures tremble in the wind
Like petty criminals unjustly hung.

Egyptian pharaoh
Watched his kittens cuddle
Few centuries ago,
We watch the sparrows
Splash water in the puddle,
Lives come and go,
Time walks the thinnest ice
Before our idle eyes.

Same pews, same churches,
Same cardinals, same urges,
Same chosen,
Same anointed ones,
Same hearts are frozen
Same singing swans.

My soul was left in care
Of psychopaths and vandals,
I'm crucified completely bare
Over the Christmas candles.

Time Will Devour Our Lives

Unless in dreams
Time never heals,
It generally seems,
We worship our ills.

I hate to fall,
You like to cry,
I wouldn't crawl,
You wouldn't fly.

Our lackluster lives
Consumed by fear,
Only amid the strives
Our paradise is near.

I'm not a coward, I can swear,
I tremble, sweating like a boar,
I have the nastiest nightmare,
I lose my courage in the war.

Few soar above the waves,
Few wipe their teary eyes,
Few cowards or few braves,
Time will devour all our lives.

All memories and sorrows,
All victories over the fears,
All our highs and lows,
Each fades and disappears.

Time

All calendars continue to shed their pages,
The only real order through the ages
And everything we know comes and goes,
But only river-time forever flows.

Time brings us from the wombs,
Time thins and colors our hairs,
Time calms and heals our sorrows,
Time cures our scars and wounds,
Time starts and stops our affairs,
Time isn't yesterdays, but tomorrows.

Time buries us...

To B.

In Holy Trinity you were the third,
I stood like a lonely wilted tree,
You landed as a painted bird,
And walked me to the end of glee.

I read and write some books,
I satisfy my curiosity and pride;
Life feels much wiser than it looks,
Life is a pleasing yet demanding ride.

Life is a golden but a falling leaf,
Life is ignoring my gloom and grief;
Life burns like candles in a sconce,
And then it simply ends at once
.

After this night
The sun will rise
Above the tide of our delight
And shine forever in your eyes.

You had a tiny magic key
From our stagnation, I still remember;
You turned that key and we flew free
Like sparks above the glowing ember.

You were a godsent morning breeze;
Without you
I live in anguish as a failing beast,
I am a lonely acrobat on a trapeze,
Without you
I am hungry at the end of every feast.

To Beth

A Russian icon of your face
Melts modestly and hides
Behind the curtains' lace,
Behind the stripes of blinds.

I'll walk across my darkest sorrow,
The lights are off on Sundays,
I hope to meet someone tomorrow,
I hope to fly in ecstasy on Mondays.

Deep anguish of my oath,
Obscurity and pain of grief,
I was a stranger to us both,
I was a swirling autumn leaf.

I left my doubts on the shelf,
I am out dancing, drinking wine,
I hope back home I will be fine,
But what if I just tease myself?

The Russian icon of your face
Gleams through the curtains' lace.

To Boris Pasternak

Young maple trees,
White virgin birches
Give purity to peace
Against our urges.

A day of spring
Brings rays of sun,
Young flowers sing,
Their shadows run.

The winds of gloomy
Battlefields
Honed our mighty
Swords,
The humans made
The shields,
Old treaties wasted
Precious words.

The valleys rest,
The rivers float,
Lie flunks the test,
Life rocks my boat.

The trees flex twigs
Wave to the strangers,
The birds stretch wings
And fly with our angels.

The brave ones
Don't come home,
They fly as dawns
Above the dome.

To Mom, Again

You lost your precious life,
You were just fifty-five,
But suddenly learned
That in a month you'd die,
For days I couldn't cry,
The bridge was burned.

You loved me
While I was a pup,
You left me
I became a dog,
I drank that cup,
Life went up in smoke.

I left behind my youth,
I've read a new prologue,
Mom, send someone
To wake me up and kiss,
I've learned the truth,
There's no other one,
I am just an ugly frog,
Turn me into a prince.

To Reinvent the Universe

The justice let me see the sky
Cut by three window bars in four;
The sun was boring like a candle,
Today, I wish I were a bird and fly
To beat the angels in a tug o' war,
And blow the unsteady sunny wick.
I bet the gods will like this scandal.

My prison seemed quite fair,
My dreams have lightened,
For years I was a little lonely,
While executors ran the drill.
I am upset, a little frightened,
The warden *pulled* the chair:
I had a single day to exit. Only!
And hastily ordered my last meal.

I wrote my final word,
I finished my last verse,
Then left this world
To reinvent the universe.

To Venice With Love

The smoke of our train
Slides to the iron trail,
I sprawl like a lazy bear
I flaunt my Russian flair.

i move from Padua to Venice,
A dictionary rests on my knees,
I talk with blue-haired women,
Dreaming of love and semen.

Late autumn, trees turned red,
The weather's folds and holds,
The old Saint Marco's spread
Locked in the cage of scaffolds.

I've been to Venice many times,
I love those never boring nights,
I love to hear St. Marco's chimes,
I love Venetian enigmatic sights.
Venetian handsome gondoliers,
Venetian old intrigues and fears,
Venetian famous coffee n' éclairs,
Murano's crystal chandeliers.
The nourished elegance of bridges,
The squeaky sounds of the oars,
The hungry nosy, loud pigeons,
The cheerful and gorgeous whores.
The music on the squares,
The spider web of the canals,
The Casanova's love affairs,
The masks of naughty carnivals.
The endless water splashes

Whisper their secrets to the walls,
The muddy waves and gushes
Sneak under the tourist's strolls.

I love Venetian nightly hazy lights,
I love Giorgione, Titian, Tintoretto,
I love the seagulls' greedy flights,
I'll write Venetian opera's libretto…

Today I Know

Today, I know,
I love to travel,
I studied maps
From end to end,
The fire or snow
Always a marvel,
A few more laps
Then I may bend.

New people, faces,
Towns, countries,
Unknown places,
Broken boundaries.

The fastest road-airline,
Few shirts and dresses,
Great dinners, wines,
Some new addresses
And yet it's always Rome
With its St. Peter's Dome.

I slowly meander over Italy,
Another day, another eatery,
Whether a giant or a gnome,
The roads lead to Rome.

I ride, I often walk or even run
My trying life is an eternal fun,
The ruined Roman Colosseum,
The modern art or a museum.

Unfortunately, I am still alone,
I have to cross that Rubicon,
Come close and hold my hand,
Our bon voyage will never end.

Today, I learned to walk

I flew like a cascade
Over the prison wall,
I fly, that's what I want to do,
I'm illicitly a red tailed hawk,
Don't ever ruin my charade,
I fly as an uprising waterfall,
I fly, that's what I always do,
I fly; I'll never crawl or walk.

Queen's "let them eat cake"
To "les miserable" have-nots,
They stormed the old Bastille,
Nobody vowed in the wake
Damn chickens in their pots
Or even a half decent meal.

Don't promise anything,
Cease rivers of your money,
Cling to your lighting dash,
Remember, you're not a king,
Just sip your milk-and-honey,
Enjoy your lovers' flash.

My lies become too friendly,
My dreams take me away,
I'll leave the horn of plenty,
Among mirages of today.

I am on the way to Guatemala,
I like Antigua's rums and coffees,
I listen to the Ninth of Mahler
It soars over the ancient coffins.

I'm bored,
The same horrific carnage,
No news under the moon,
My lord,
Get some real knowledge
From these natives, soon.

I am a wingless hawk,
Today, I learned to walk,
One basket for all eggs
Until my final breath,
I am walking on my pegs,
I try to outsmart my death.

Tomorrow and Today

You were so beautiful,
I was a drunken fool,
Tomorrow,
I'll quit, I'll be sober,
Tomorrow,
I'll quit, It will be over,
Tomorrow,
You'll be still beautiful,
Tomorrow,
I'll be just a sober fool.

I'm the same forever,
Time breaks its mold,
Time turns its lever,
Today,
You are not beautiful,
Today,
You are quite old,
Today,
I'm still a drunken fool.

Tomorrow, I'll Embrace Sunshine

Another star dies in the sky,
I hear the howl of a proud wolf,
The clouds softly whisper bye,
The moon smirks on the roof.

Autumn relearns to dance the Waltz,
Dry yellow leaves swirl in the grass,
Pale shadows stroll across the walls,
Obedient as children going to their class.

Life is a fragile thread,
Short as a cradlesong,
It's closer to the end,
Which I'm determined to prolong.

The turbid wine of my existence
Is timely roiled
By a divine persistence
In being totally eschewed
From the unspoiled
Innocence of fallen angels
Disguised as passing strangers.

You called me on the phone,
Tonight, your smile is in my wine,
I'm in pain; I'd like to be alone,
Tomorrow, I'll embrace sunshine.

Tomorrow

I gasped a mouthful of air,
I reached the tunnel's end,
There wasn't honey for a bear,
There was no beam of light.

Jack Daniels, my bosom friend
Would taste quite good tonight.

I'll drink this amber sunny nectar,
Amusement of my distant youth,
For us it was a lie-detector
Demanding truth and only truth.

Even the broken clocks
Are perfectly correct
Two times a day.
Tomorrow never knocks,
It's not yet wrecked,
Tomorrow's here to stay.

Tomorrow,
I'll see a murky yellow spot,
But write my verses to the sun.
Tomorrow,
I'll slash the Gordian knot,
You'll hear my farewell plea,
You'll watch my last homerun,
You'll enjoy my final apogee.

Tonight, I Take No Calls

I dream of what I could
Accomplish in my play,
I'm always in the mood,
To please a lovely prey.

I told a preacher
In a formal cloak;
"You are a teacher,
You can walk and talk,
Why do we camouflage
Our naughty dreams,
Why do we sabotage
Our delicious whims?"

Here's my latest one:
I'm in Moscow, a day's gone,
Red Square with red sunset,
I try to squeeze my hammer
Through her gorgeous sickle,
A Russian girl says "nyet",
She shows me her glamour,
I am showing her my pickle.

My Russian international affair
Allowed me to make my nickel,
I earned her tender, loving care,
I know what to do, I am not fickle.

Tonight, I take no calls,
I am completely freed
From worthless goals,
I have arrived to breed.

Too Early

A very few can entertain my interest
Considerably longer than a day,
And my fine-timed emotional unrest
Looks for a noiseless harbor far away.

Our love of life is not a meditation,
It molds and nourishes our formation;
Our souls and bodies fly into the blue
Then luckily descend as something new.

It isn't hard to like and buy a work of art,
There are so many hand-mixed colors,
Only a creativity inborn in every heart
Cannot be bought for millions of dollars.

The readers pessimistic observations
Are driven by my honest indignations,
I am continuously torn between two roles,
The truths and lies performing on the poles.

There is a wise and gentle man,
A conscious jailbird inside of me,
But I don't let him talk;
It is too early to reveal my plan:
I'll never ask to be or not to be,
I'll learn to fly, I'll be free,
I'll become a red-tailed hawk.

Too Late to Weep

There're only a few
With whom I'd like to sleep,
But very, very few
With whom I'd like to wake
And wake again in love,
Forever fresh and deep.
To whom I'd wave goodbye,
But miss and long for her
Not knowing why.
With whom I'd love to dream
Or silently enjoy white clouds
Competing in the blue
And whisper, "I love you".

Before our castle fell apart,
Why didn't we learn to seal it?
Before you broke my heart,
Why didn't you learn to heal it?
We haven't left a single stone
Unturned,
The remnants left, we earned.
I genuinely loved, but learned
No coming back. The bridge
Was burned.

The past was trained
By our tomorrows,
Our love was chained
To pain of sorrows.

It is too late to weep
And rake the beads.
It is a time to reap
The ripened deeds.

Too Late

Don't give me your stump speech,
Too late, you cannot win me over,
You crossed and burned the bridge,
The river on my side moves slower.

The lottery's wrong numbers,
The old and melting snow,
A great ballplayer fumbles
After a weak or timid throw.

The flame of a trembling candle
Left darkness, carved your face,
You sit at the dining table
With meek somebody else.

It's not the time to reap,
It is too late to sow,
Your journey is a sour trip
The end of which I know.

Too Many Candles

The fire of scandals
In the wake
Of glow,
Too many candles
On my cake
To blow.

The autumn of my life,
I run across the steppe,
I badly need another day,
The miles are still ahead,
The leaded clouds wept
Under the Milky Way,
I'll return when I'm dead.

My mind has outlived
My flesh,
My flesh has outlived
My mind,
My memory is fresh,
My intellect is blind.

I used to like sunrise,
Today, I liked sunset,
I tossed the lucky dice,
My fortune said not yet.

My road to nowhere,
The past is dwarfed,
A circle is a square,
Reality is morphed.

My stubborn pain,
A very heavy toll,
I dreamed in vain,
Goodbye, my soul.

Too Many Girls

Too many girls
Were never kissed,
Too many barrels
Wait to be uncorked,
Few golden curls
Will not be missed,
The church's carols
Still never worked.

The Sundays come and go,
The crosses shine and glow,
In vain, we built the church,
A symbol of eternal search.

To save the boys, at least,
We will defrock the priests
Or even better yet,
Allow them to wed.

Although, above the fray,
Our angels hover near,
Just a handshake away,
Let's change the gear.

Too Many Voices

Too many voices,
One gloomy vision,
Too many choices,
One wrong decision.

The latter or the former,
The ducks already lined,
I see beyond the corner,
I cannot change my mind.

My granny's violets
Were burned in war,
Her cozy garden died,
The past is violent,
I slammed the door,
I left my youth behind.

The dramas never learn,
We walk the thawed ice,
New spring has sprung,
The bridges sadly burn,
The winter shut its eyes,
The memory has swung.

I bark, but cannot bite,
I cannot fight much longer
I have misplaced my might,
My enemies are stronger,
They arrogantly march
Under Triumphal arch.

The comedies don't learn,
They're as tragedies return.

Too Many Years

Too many years,
Too many miles,
Too many fears,
Too many lies...

Those, who never hated,
Will never learn to love,
But those, who waited
Won't ever have enough.

We are two poles
Of our planet Earth,
We play the roles
Of parted twins at birth.

I kissed your cherry lips,
I plundered your surprise,
I know why the cupid weeps,
You are Venus in disguise.

You are my shiny dream,
Let's thread the needle,
I want our love to gleam,
I'll sing, I'll play my fiddle.

Are you a castle in the sky?
Are you a foggy quiet lake?
Are you a bird, trying to fly?
Am I asleep, am I awake?

I fought, I strived
For many years,
I finally arrived
To love and cheers.

Toward Our Vague Tomorrows

Our conscience marches
Under triumphant arches,
Toward the pits of sorrows
Toward our vague tomorrows.

We lose our belief in Gods and people,
We gather under each church's steeple
The faded shadows of our fallen friends,
Absorb pathetic in-the-know trends,
Then quietly descend without any names
Into the quagmires of our uncertain aims.

The recollections never seem to hold
What our broken hearts reject,
Our valuables are quickly sold,
And our relationships are wrecked.

Even the longest twine must end,
Even the strongest people bend.
The old railroads are too shaky
For blissfully smooth tomorrows,
My principles are dead or flaky,
Only my poetry still shily flows.

The epitaph won't fade
From my tombstone:
"He was betrayed,
And died of that aversion.
Confess, he wasn't alone
In this eventual excursion."

Triumphant Nike

The darkest night falls
Into the palms of dusk,
My inner demon calls,
He wants to peel my husk.

The history repeats itself,
New tragedies destroy
The vaudevilles of lives,
Old comedies forever shelf
The tales of endless strives.

Dense shadows of my edgy days,
Loom fearlessly above my nights,
My sleepless, needy body craves
The self-indulging "Garden of delights".

Great Bosch entices my nomadic mind,
Although, rejects my soul:
The blind still cruelly leads the blind
Into a more attractive hole.

I am the densest olden ice
I loathe the rites of springs;
I shut the door and turned the key,
Then for a minute closed my eyes;

Triumphant goddess Nike
Unfurled her mighty wings.

Truth Leaves No Trace

I prized my gentle youth,
It really wasn't worth it,
I feared the naked truth,
I wore a suit to clothe it.

I loathed the living
In the killing fields,
I wasn't ever willing
To collect the yields.

Naïve, but truly wise
In the pursuit of truth,
I hunted in disguise
Of curiosity and youth.

Experimenting truth
Sets free our nihilism,
A disappearing youth
Delivers conformism.

I wear a scar of grief
On my unruffled face,
Youth is a falling leaf,
Truth leaves no trace.

Truths Have No Colors

My train has left the station,
I gathered nothing to forget,
My intellect wasn't a fruit of
education,
Great education was a fruit
of intellect.

Truths have no colors,
Just black and white,
Lies look like rainbows
Above the bad and worse,
Above the wrong and right,
Above the sun and frost;
My guiding star still glows,
My revelation won't get lost
Between the sun and frost.

I wrote
A book of melancholy,
A book of war and peace,
I brought
Into this world my folly,
Forgive me, please.

We fought at dusk and dawn,
We fought behind the doors,
We fought in front of everyone,
We fought our unending wars.

The blind went to the ditch,
We lost another war,
Warmongers turn the switch,
New war knocks on the door.

Crème de la crème,
The golden fleece
Of a winged ram
Can't rest in peace.

Twelve

Twelve epigones of your affairs,
Twelve pigeon-chested heirs
Caressing pride and vanity in thee,
Cajoling you to change the world,
To walk across the sea of Galilee
And justify your father's word.

The same old dirty politics,
I've heard when someone said,
I'll be judged by the same twelve,
Then carried by the chosen six
Into my cold, but comfy rocky bed.

When you will come to visit me
Before the twelve o'clock midnight,
I'll be delirious, but I'll humbly plea,
"Forgive my yet another sin,
Allow me to see the rays of light,
I long for you and Mary Magdalene."

Another day has nearly gone,
Twelve hours before next dawn.
I'm treading water of the sea
Of learning,
I see twelve marching shadows
On the beach,
Sunset of ignorance is burning,
Casing its bloody light on each.

Two Actors Left the Stage

The beauty n' the beast,
You were a masterpiece,
Magnificent and proud,
You were a happy dawn,
I was a miserable cloud,
Those days have gone.

The star of our brittle love
While smolders far above,
Won't guide us anymore,
The end waits at the door.

The drops of morning dew
Spark in your brown eyes,
It was a final night with you,
It's time to say goodbye.

We drank enough
The wines of love,
Today, we're sober,
We know, it is over.

The honey of your kiss,
The almonds of your eyes,
I savored all these years
Dark truths and shiny lies.

A pile of legal paper clips,
The bitter chocolate of life,
Its flavor lingers on my lips,
Tonight, you were my wife.

My heart is someplace else,
Our love won't start again,
I think, you'll never guess,

I left you on the other train,
The page of love is burned,
The verses have returned
Into the olden gloomy cage,
Two actors left the stage.

Two Autumn Leaves Fell on my Shoulders

Two autumn leaves fell on my shoulders,
They look like golden outdated epaulets
As on the brown photographs of soldiers.
It's almost dusk; I walk my naughty pets.

My neighbors ride their sparkly bikes,
Run with the earphones on their heads
Or hold their phones, chat to the mikes,
And laughing loudly like newlyweds.

I praise my unassuming neighborhood:
After my sleepless excruciating nights,
It brings me back into a pleasant mood
From my nightmares of wars and fights.

Dark nights engender falling stars,
I try, in vain, to find them and cease,
Drinking with my buddies in the bars,
At times, with help of love and peace.

Two autumn leaves fall on my shoulders,
They gleam like ancient golden epaulets
Adorning weathered faces of the vets
On faded out photographs of soldiers.

I light two candles, then curse the nights;
My soul surrenders to my enduring fights.

The Chair of Monsieur Voltaire

Delightful Left Bank of Paris,
I cross the busy Latin quarters,
As loud as the empty rolling barrels
In custody of the worldly trotters.

I stop in front of Le Procope,
There is an object of my hope:
A celebrated ancient armchair
Which hosted Francois Voltaire.

A Maître d' was not surprised,
But asked an outrageous price;
I paid; he pulled the famous chair
Much loved by Monsieur Voltaire.

I comfortably sunk into the pillow,
A waiter bent like a weeping willow,
I ordered wine, a five-course dinner,
I am an epicure; I am a happy sinner,
I am dining in a three-century old chair
Appreciated by the butt of great Voltaire.

Two Daughters

I can't erase my happy grin,
In front of me my lovely girls
Victoria and Katherine,
Two priceless pearls.

Long shadows on the grass
Are cast by the leafless tree,
They look like the prison's bars,
They separate my girls and me.

Life's enigmatic art
Throws them apart,
Two lovely daughters
In the muddy waters.

The ships are sinking,
Into unanswered love,
No one is thinking
Of saying "That's enough."

The seagulls fly away,
Two captains bravely stay,
The truth and peace may die,
Only their pride may know why.

Two Feisty Noisy Ravens

Two feisty noisy ravens
Chase a red-tailed hawk
Into the heavens…
I watch and walk.

There's always time
To do just nothing,
Chisel a better rhyme
Or wait for something.

The river dries,
The angels fall,
The devil flies,
Days slowly crawl.

I am quite wise but immature,
I am a paranoid wonk, no cure,
I have a picture-perfect ploy:
After the hell will freeze,
I'll certainly enjoy
My rest in peace.

Two Friends

One blinding flare,
Two waterfalls of glee,
Two locks of silver hair,
One diamond jubilee.

Time strolls,
Two friends,
Two gentle souls
Still holding hands.

A closing page,
End of the rope,
Young hearts, old age,
Only a tender hope,
One wish; two friends
Still holding hands.

Two humble forces,
Two gentle verses,
Two loving friends
Still holding hands.

The final terminal,
The end of rails,
Nobody drives,
Axiomatic formula
Which never fails,
The end of lives.

Two trembling hands
Of our lifelong trial,
Two marching bands
New Orleans' style.

The end of lifelong sparkly rails,
We flaunt our departure smiles,
Somebody drives two final nails,
Our coffins walk two extra miles.

Two Halves of Me

A morning coffee's brew,
Instead of mother's milk,
I played and outgrew
The cradle's lacy silk.

Parisian walkways
Of Gary Moore,
A hymn of acid days,
Merci, no more.

My psychedelic views,
Were rainbows after rain,
I gave my poetry in vain
To those who had no clue.

My world has oddly changed,
The trees went underground,
The clouds are entrenched,
Sun wrongly rolls eastbound.

Instead of a dinner suit,
I wear a backless cloak,
The nurse is really cute,
The rest are crazy folk.

The bridge is burned
Between two halves of me,
One half has no desire to flee,
The other longs for being free,
This one has earned
To dance with dawns of glee.

Two halves don't ever fight,
There is no wrong or right.

Two Lonesome Stars

A single napkin
For two eaters,
A second captain
On a sinking ship,
Two eager hitters
Can't share a grip.

Disaster of the smart,
Unification fell apart,
Two yet unwilling hearts
Missed by the cupid's darts.

Two actors in disguise,
Two stars can't share a stage,
The same earsplitting cries,
The same exaggerated rage.

There are no fits and starts:
Two lonely stubborn hearts
Can't cross the stream
Of their forgotten dream.

Only the strings of rain
Try to caress their pain;
Only the rainbows loom
Over impenetrable gloom.

Two Stars

A single napkin
For two eaters,
A second captain
On a little ship,
Two eager hitters
Can't share a grip.

Disaster of the smart,
Our ship is decked,
Our house fell apart,
Our family is wrecked

Two actors in disguise,
Two stars, only one stage,
Same earsplitting cries,
Same theatre of the rage.

Two Wedding Rings

Two wedding rings,
Two total strangers,
Two pairs of wings,
Two flying angels,
Two birds in bliss,
Two naked souls,
Two major roles,
A single kiss.

Another short affair,
Another losing hand,
Another parting pair,
Another funeral jazz band,
Another line to heaven,
Another set mortal seven.

Two lonely strangers,
Two wingless angels…

Two Wingless Doves

We showered with gold,
No bitter losses, only wins,
We didn't break the mold,
We drowned in those sins.

A day passed by and died,
We walk through our night,
We try to leave our past,
We freely breathe, at last.

We reap the fruits we sow,
Laughter deserts our room,
A silent devastating blow
Wraps our lives in gloom.

We hide from modern trends
Between the virgin pages
Of our yet unwritten books,
We dwell in unfamiliar lands,
We give our bloody wages
To cloaked conniving crooks
Under the church's gables,
They see two wingless doves,
They tease us with the fables
About glory of eternal loves.

An angel of tomorrows,
A toddler yet unborn
Will wash our sorrows
With music of his horn.

Two Women in my Life

Two women in my life
My mother and my wife,
The price of real love
Is never high enough.
I passed the bars,
I wore the cloak,
I saw the stars,
They lit my walk.

I'm jailed, I am insane,
I rip my soul to pieces,
I soar above the rain,
Their hugs and kisses.
The nightly sparkly stars,
Revealed my hiding place,
I'm chained behind the bars,
After their last embrace.

My heartless guard,
Don't hide your eyes,
Perform your deadly art,
My soul already flies.
He didn't aim,
He didn't miss,
No one to blame,
I went to bliss.
Two women in my life
My mother and my wife,
The price of real love
Is never high enough.

Two

We are two homeless hearts,
We are two souls with doubts,
We are two abandoned carts
By careless shopping crowds.

Life drains us almost dry
And, yet, it leaves enough
In us of a necessity to fly,
Enough to madly fall in love.

Our eyes have met tonight,
We knew unspoken invitations,
Our manners veiled desires,
Our lips were rather tight.
Two waiting trains, two stations,
Two beings, two hidden fires.

We stood only a step away
From ragged edges of a bluff.
We didn't jump into the play,
We were afraid to fall in love.

Two lives, two parallels,
Two lives, two equal parts,
Two shiny rails, two ends,
Two pasts, two injured hearts,
Two joyless losses,
Two crucifixion-ready crosses.

Under the Rainbow

Life is eternal almanac:
The winter of my life
Gave me the spring;
I greatly miss my wife,
She gave me back
Her wedding ring.

The watercolor streams
Across my vivid dreams
And washes them away,
But lets the past to stay.

My aspirations fly
Under the rainbow,
The birds are high
Along the river flow.
Don't ask me why
I sit in the first row

It's not the end;
I caught some fish,
And told my newest friend,
Bring me a serving dish.
Relax, enjoy and all the rest,
Here's the music, take a seat,
I promise, I'll do my very best,
I'll sip my beer and grill.
It's not an inexpensive lure;
If you won't drink and eat,
I'm absolutely sure,
The second mouse will.

It is my banner to unfurl,
My favorite whorehouse,
Great brandy and striptease;
I picked another lovely girl,
She was the second mouse,
She got the luscious cheese.

Under the Sails Unfurled

Love is my daily bread,
I live by love alone,
If sensuality is dead,
Reality is left to moan.

There is no side to take,
There is the past,
There are tomorrows,
Loves hardly ever outlast
The memory of sorrows.

My life isn't carefree,
I try to navigate its sea
Under the sails unfurled,
To destiny I have deserved.

There are no ways to find out
If there is somebody I can trust,
I'll take my chances if I must
Amid the homeless hereabout.

My writing is a bloody sport,
It takes my verses as a token
Of loves that thrown overboard,
My heart still bleeds, it's broken.

The apathy embraced my planet,
I am utterly confused and hiding
Under the quilt of a moral vomit,
Behind the ensued evil's guiding.

Unexpected Worries

A war is over but I still fight for peace,
For both the gander and for the geese.
My Holy Bible wrapped in cellophane,
Today, I am self-satisfied and calm
Like nature after a devastating rain,
Like Mathew's "Our Father..." psalm.

A dark rectangle of the door
Is a reminder of everything I miss:
My breezy youth which is no more,
And my loving Mother I forgot to kiss.

I am Orestes threatened by the Furies
Personifying anger of the dead;
I am burdened by unexpected worries
About our godsent daily bread:
A harsh coldblooded mind
Of a fallen wingless angel,
Wrote yet another testament,
Quite masterfully intertwined
That glorifies a moneychanger.

A living is a toughest choice
While between Scylla and Charybdis;
We wisely listen to our inner voice
And try to guess the lesser of two evils.

Life is a dusk
Between nirvana and despair;
Life is a dawn
Between our misery and glee;
I live, the rest is just a husk;
When life is playing chess,
I definitely am not a pawn.

Unknown Routes

I walk unknown routes,
My weighty backpack
Filled with hazy doubts,
I picked along my track.
A never-ending day,
A never-ending rope,
A blinding sunny ray.
A glimpse of hope.

Indian Territory,
I am an uninvited guest,
Tense, but consolatory,
Trying to do my best;
A long sheathed knife
Is dangling from my belt,
I entered an eccentric life
With odds I have been dealt.

I drowned in chagrin,
Uneasy and annoyed,
I have committed sin,
I boldly broke the rules
And went into the void
Into the world of fools.

I saw with my own eyes,
Once-in-a-lifetime debut:
Under tumultuous skies
A new moonchild is born,
Predestined to the fame,
A pure white baby bison.
The chiefs, the chosen few
Gave him a relished name,
No one on Earth yet worn,
"Heavenly Father's liaison".

Unnecessary Sin

We are admired for the myths,
That built our houses of cards,
Filled with the haze of fables,
Stacked with the silky wreaths
Obtained for our graveyards,
But pushed to sky-high gables.

Life is a dungeon. We're jailed,
All those who wouldn't preach,
All those who tried, but failed,
All kind and vulnerable souls
That soared, but couldn't reach
Their countless idealistic goals.

The eighth unnecessary sin,
A truly necessary evil,
Lived in a memory's dustbin.
It didn't want to shrivel,
It didn't deserve to live or die.
Its soul was quickly mopped,
And just a single passer-by
Has innocently stopped
To wave the last goodbye.

A sour voice of our warden
Barks orders to the guards,
Wet quilts of our boredom
Mute songs of jailed bards.

The eighth and yet unknown sin,
Will never die; it left the litterbin.

Unreasonably Tortured

My passionate style of living,
My clean uncluttered space
Where I rejoice the glee of being,
And friends of mine deserve a place,
Unquestionably fits the bill;
I'm certain they'll appreciate the thrill.

Despair of countless years
Has melted with a winter's snow;
The innocence of an early spring
Brought music to my ears
On wings of a morning blow;
Full-throated birds began to sing.

Flamboyant and intense,
Unreasonably tortured
Depiction of reality
Have never tried to help me
To introduce a common sense
Or heal a psychological duality
Of those who hold the rusty key
From our future poorly nurtured.

My thoughts are heralded
By thinly nuanced layers
Of ancient doubts and conclusions
Made by the baffled players
Who veer within their own illusions
About buried souls of the flying dead.

A comedy became a tragedy
I couldn't cease my grief;
There is no cure, no remedy:
Death doesn't wait. Life is too brief.

Unsung

I kept my often-idle eyes and ears
Completely open to the lies rehearsed,
I lost too many precious years,
I am still alive; I guess I am reimbursed.

Late night,
I watch the river like a well-fed python
Lazily crawls under a hunchback-bridge;
I write…
It is about time to turn the night-light on,
And pull my TV dinner from the fridge.

Life is like a deadly boring anecdote;
It seems too long when you are young;
Although, it seems much longer
When every song you ever wrote
Is still unsung.

A psychological meltdown
Of our fragile paradigm
Reminds me of a wedding gown
Acquired for a bogus dime.

I can't not write my lines,
I have to straighten all the bowed spines
Of those whose problems are too heavy,
Of those who can't afford to have a levee.

Until I Tossed My Dice

I grew up as a curious boy,
I saw the sunsets of denial,
Life was an enigmatic ploy,
I saw the banners of desire
Soared high above the lake
As hearts before they break.

Once my grandmother said:
"While you are still a child
Take care of your fresh mind
You will be forever living with,
To know good from bad,
To know truth from myth."

I've never had a clue
Until I tossed my dice,
And only then I knew
The virtue from the vise.

Until the Mud Was Thrown

The fiery nights seem
Darker
Above the silhouettes
Of tanks,
The rockets gleam
And sparkle,
We hide, while they
Pull ranks.

Deaths fly from
Unexpected corners
And sail across
The sea of mourners.

Over atrocities revealed,
We pull our futile covers,
In vain, I try to shield
Those naked horrors.

Foes cast a stone,
I answer with a rock,
The sad result is known,
Life is a butcher's block.

My coffee cup
Remains half full,
I am asked: "What's up?"
I say: "Just push and pull."

I tried to fool my death,
I hid the grave I own,
I cherished every breath
Until the mud was thrown.

The date of birth
Carved on my tomb,
The date of death
Locked in the womb.

Unwanted Gift

When youth is gone,
They try to bring it back
With cheap cosmetics,
Or bourgeois aesthetics.

There are not too many
With whom I am happy to wake up;
I'd rather save a penny,
On greedy lawyers to break us up.

I like to be alone,
At times, life is a twilight zone:
The fingertips of rain
Loudly knocking on my roof
Their wild cacophony of pain;
I am sipping wine; I am bulletproof.

I never have much time
To sip my wine and write;
It is my punishment without crime,
A lifelong leap into a divinity of light.

A breezy morning gifted me
A pleasing sense of hope;
I mumbled one, two, three,
And stepped on my tightrope,
A tightrope of my fated drift,
A dreadful and yet unwanted gift.

Upended Days

My world capsized,
It's upside-down,
I only now realized,
I used to be a king.
Today, I am a clown.

I lost my optimistic sight,
I gambled with my skin,
I took it on the chin,
And lost my final fight

The nights upended days,
More comfort for the blind,
There are no other ways,
Some lose, the others find.

A nation of shopkeepers,
Of borrowers and lenders,
Of homeless house flippers,
And morbid sex-offenders;
Forget your loud jeers,
Don't lie, you're not deaf,
Give me your idle ears,
Here are the rules; I am a ref.

Please, listen; pay attention,
Ben Franklin was quite sure,
"An ounce of prevention
Is worth a pound of cure."

I begged for help my muse,
She sent a futile horoscope,
I sensed the endless blues,
She offered grief, not hope.

Utopian Desire

Far-fetched Utopian desire
To live forever after death,
Reminds me of an amplifier
For someone's final breath.

I am alive. Long live the fall;
I am alive. Nights fly, days stroll;
The air above is crisp, bone-dry,
Leaves turn into a yellow brass,
Red-tiled roofs beam in the sky
Like ripened apples in blue grass.

It takes a while to overcome
My stagnant skepticism,
To energize my brain
Covered with a wet blanket
Of an outdated nihilism,
To organize a lavish banquet,
And hear my real voice again.

Rejections are too hard
To disregard. I am a bard,
I am a poet drowning in wine,
Serving a lifelong sentence,
Stroppy deceits' acceptance
Sends chills down my spine.

The boundaries are blurred
Between integrity and laws
It's our retaliation in disguise,
It's our logic and the absurd
Of freedoms and death rows
Among the virtue and the vice.

Far-fetched Utopian desire
To live forever after death,
Reminds me of an amplifier
For someone's final breath.

Van Cliburn

Old Russia in the fifties,
The Cold War's almost hot,
Van Cliburn crossed the t's
Then every i received a dot.

The First Tchaikovsky competition,
The ancient Steinway slightly worn,
Van played; a man was on a mission,
It was a miracle, the star was born.

The angels were descending,
He closed his eyes and played,
The sounds were ascending,
This memory will never fade.

The sacred pantheon of glory,
The grandeur of ovations,
He played into the history
For yet unknown generations.

The avalanche of flowers
Fell on the famous stage
They were my happiest hours
I know something at my age.

I met my hero, good old Van,
In Texas, a few years ago,
I shook his hand as a devout fan,
We kindly spoke about Moscow,
Emotions, doubts, the first prize,
I saw teardrops in his blue eyes.

Van Gogh

The orange sun is wet,
The yellow sky has flu,
Even the clouds sweat,
Our Vincent sees the blue,
An artist is a fragile cup,
An artist falls and breaks
Into mosaic on the floor,
We quickly glue it up,
Few scars, few aches,
For us it's not enough,
We are demanding more,
We want him to be tough.

Sunflowers sadly died,
The brushes rolled aside,
Poor Vincent lives in fear,
Estranged and mocked,
A whore receives his ear
Before he is locked up,
Pain helps to create,
A suffering is blessed,
He couldn't fool his fate,
Art never left his chest.

He's heaven bound,
To hug his starry night
Above the guilty ground
Into the never-ending light,
His art so vividly defies
The critics' devil's craft,
They closed their eyes
To miss his blinding shaft.

Van Gogh has gone,
He brushed away,
Another mourning dawn
Starts yet another a day.

Venetian Air

Am I too gullible? Am I still wrong?
My memory hides multitudes of sins,
Nobody wants to share my laughter,
Nobody wants to hear my final song,
My priest as always spills the beans.
Tonight, I'll write my farewell chapter.

Everyone's life ends up in death,
Most seldom try to live uniquely,
The angels wait for our final breath,
And let us vanish rather quickly.

Again, the rite of spring,
Venetian air is trembling
Above the rolling waves
So crudely interrupted
By noisy passing boats.

A dissonance of memories,
A harmony of lovely sights,
Crossing the boundaries
Of unprecedented grandeur,
And acquaints us with glory.
.
I come to Venice every spring
To navigate within my past,
And lull whatever is still left.
I see an old man
Every time I shave,
I see a frightened sinner,
A pale clone of a burlesque.

While I am writing final pages,
At dusk I met a gorgeous girl,
She didn't compare our ages,
She saw me a real winner,
Just slightly Kafkaesque.

Venus

You are a taker not a giver,
Cold as a broken heart,
Left on the beach to shiver,
Knowing that love is art.

You are not a goddess,
You'll never be an angel,
You are a slave of love,
Cold, heartless stranger
Deprived of fondness,
You never have enough.

A masterpiece of youth,
A naked piece of truth;
You were introduced
As Neptune's daughter
Wrapped in the sun,
Caressed by water;
I am willingly seduced,
To worship you till dawn.

Victorious Defeat

Victorious defeat
Of our joyless love,
We die on our feet,
We live by our bluff.

You nicely make our bed,
You like this nightly chore,
But then you always beg
To treat you like a whore.

Please, never send me
A silly thank you note,
Please, set me free,
Don't rock my boat.

I have a second thought,
It is your second chance;
Wear a new dress I bought
Come close, let's dance.

Let's have and eat the cake,
You are a comfy snowfall,
You are a frail snowflake,
Don't melt, just bare it all,
Then do the nightly chore,
I'll treat you like a whore.

Voluptuary Wife

The heart of Burgundy, old Beaune,
For lunch I had Boeuf Bourguignon
A pricey bottle of La Tache Pinot Noir,
I thanked in French: "Merci, Au revoir."

For a traditional late dinner
My escargot came as a winner,
Before a luscious Coq Au Vin
With my beloved Chambertin.

My morning omelet was insane,
Few gulps of great Champagne
Chased by Oeuf en Meurette
And coffee with a fresh baguette.

I crave my epicurean tomorrow,
A beastly appetite I never borrow,
My luscious eats are not a trend,
It is my sybaritic life until the end;
My voyages, my meals and wine
Are heavenly, they're just divine.

I am a host, I am a guest,
It is my gastronomic quest,
I guzzle, wolf, even devour,
I never let my food go sour,
I am married to a lavish life,
It is my dear voluptuary wife.

Wait for Me, Please.

Ferocious pain,
Depressing loss,
No one to blame,
I drag my cross.

It's not the end,
I'll see the light,
It's just a dent,
I'll win the fight.

Wait for me, please.

I'll stop the rain,
I'll calm your fears,
I'll cease my pain,
I'll wipe your tears.

What doesn't kill me
Makes me stronger,
Without you I am not free,
Without you I only wonder.

Wait for me, please.

Love is a consecrated word,
You are my fragile whim,
In every corner of the world,
Love fills me to the rim.

We pick an eagle or a dove,
Eternity of war and peace,
I am forever yours, my love.

Just let me find you, please.

War is Hell

Humiliated and unmasked,
At the beginning of all ends,
To save our souls, we're asked
To be disloyal to our fallen friends.

My life was like a train,
I rode alone without a friend,
Toward the dead but happy end.
Under the weight of daily life,
In vain,
I tried to catch a falling knife.

Today, I am on my own,
My life is in my hands,
I blow my own horn
Without marching in the bands.

The autumns chill my soul,
The winters freeze my heart,
And yet I reached my goal,
My life looks like a work of art.

My fallen friends don't gather
When listen to "Our Father...
Or hear, "You'll meet His Son...
They made that hole-in-one.

We never count scars
Of our fallen angels;
We only count falling stars
Or calmly passing strangers;
We turn our heads,
We take the bait,
And make some crazy wishes

Then wait
In front empty dishes
For earthly paradise,
But never recognize
That our fallen never rise.

Waterfalls of Vanity

I sing to earn my beer,
Smoke hides the bar,
Nobody wants to hear
The cries of my guitar.

Bartender, tell the naked truth,
Straight as the strings of rain;
I suffered greatly in my youth,
Do I deserve a day without pain?

My dreams are perfectly designed,
They never heard about gravity;
They entertain my soul and mind
With tempting waterfalls of vanity.

My nightmares stay in bed,
I can enjoy my morning ride,
Yet I am hanging by a thread
Of interwoven vanity and pride.

I'll ignore the warning signs,
I'll navigate the twilight zone,
I'll dream between the lines,
But carve my poetry in stone.

We Are Just Strangers, Both of Us

Neither the sinners, nor the saints,
We are just strangers, both of us,
We fly like gracious regal cranes,
And have no problems to discuss.

The blanket of a starry night
Hides our secrets in the flight,
And from the zenith of the skies,
The moon reflects in our eyes.

Life is a futile, vulgar farce,
We are two total strangers,
Two shadows on the grass,
Straight as the prison bars,
We are two blind avengers
Dump gold but collect brass.

We Are Religious Enough to Hate

An old salt sailor is a fatalist,
My name is always on that list,
A sailor never learns to swim,
He counts on his fate and whim.

He doesn't go up to face the end,
He doesn't fly; he only goes down,
An angel knows where he went,
He'll watch the stars and drown.

I love the hookers and the sailors,
The storytellers and the strippers,
The rest of us are boring failures,
We are the seas without ripples.

I've read again the Book of Life,
My heroes die; the cowards thrive.
I've read a page after a page,
And locked my demons in the cage.

Our innocence falls for the bait,
Our prides will never stop to bluff,
We are religious enough to hate,
But not enough to love…

We Both Are Wrong

Two needles and no thread
Across cacophony of years
In search of our daily bread,
We faced the walls of fears.

We learned a lot,
Forgot much more,
We found our slot,
But lost our shore.

Love never dies,
The quiet night
Hides our sighs,
We do what's right,
We write our song,
New day is bright,
We both are wise,
We both are wrong.

Life is a merciless battlefield,
Our wounds are never healed;
We throw a useless bait
To hungry swirling sharks,
We learn to navigate
Without buoys or marks.

We Fought the Hordes

We fought the hordes
Of dedicated warriors,
Ignoring desert breeze;
Their vicious warlords
Discarded our worries
About war and peace.

We won the war,
We lost the peace,
No one could find
The Golden fleece.
My buddies died,
They failed to soar,
They rest in peace.
Their preachers lied.
My sadness blames
Their clever verses,
Their flashy claims,
Their sugared curses.

War shut too many doors,
I miss my fallen friends,
They saw the battles' ends,
They saw the end of wars.

I used to have two wings,
But burned them in this war,
Which lasts too many springs,
But no one ever kept the score.

We Grieve

War digs for them six feet
Under the frozen ground;
For boys, who had to cheat
To buy a whiskey round.

A strong yet stupid bird
Buries her head in sand,
We laugh at the absurd,
Don't be that bird, my friend.

A grieving mother cries;
She lost her boy at war.
His soul flies in the skies,
God's keeping score.

Like we, some time before,
With posters in our hands,
Chanted, make love, not war!
Bring peace unto our lands!

Damn Washington D.C.,
Up to its eyes in mud,
As far, as we can see
The city's red with blood
Of those whom we admire,
Of our sons and daughters,
They vanish in the fire,
You brought upon us.

It's written, Gods forgive.
We never do. We grieve.

We Laughed Through Our Days

We fought for our rights,
We laughed through
Our troubled days,
We danced through
Our happy nights,
Forever give-and-take,
We knew no other ways,
Our future's in the make.

Our lives remind me
Of a zebra's stripes:
Some days are black
As our dreary nights,
Some nights are white
As our virgin brides.

Life is a spinning wheel,
It turns; it's never still.
Today you're on top,
Tomorrow it's a flop.

Come close, pragmatic friends,
Here are much better trends,
A total freedom with no love
A sober life of a devoted dove.

I open wide my golden cage,
I am much wiser at my age,
My bird of hope soars high,
Away into the endless sky.

When you return,
My lovely thing,
Bring my naïve
And careless youth,
Leave lies behind
Bring nothing,
But the truth.

I search the labyrinth of years,
I find only boredom when I look,
I store the knowledge of my tears
Between the pages of my book.

We Live Among this Fraud

We live among this fraud,
Faked useless gallantries,
Banality of a plastic world,
Between the plastic trees.

We know what to say,
We know what to wear,
We suffer all the way
As much as we can bear.

Crossfire of our stares,
Reflected by the floors,
We polish our affairs,
We laundry our souls.

Don't stay too long,
Don't be too loud,
They'll know you belong
If you're hazy as a cloud.

I'll write and sing for you
About our love and fights,
About elixirs of morning dew,
About passions of the nights.

We Live; Thus, It Is Bliss

Don't hate,
Just disobey the brass,
And wait;
Cease fire, don't yield,
Don't take that bait
Until the gentle grass
Covers the battlefield.

The dawns will glow,
The flowers will grow,
Just think how fair life is,
We live; thus, it is bliss.

We Longed for Glee

Spellbinding tale
Of ancient bards
For every season,
For Hell and paradise,
For sunny days or hale.
Tongue-lashing guards
Locked me in prison,
Lifecycle rolls the dice.

A leaded cloud weeps,
Small town hits the sack,
My prison never sleeps,
The night is scary black.

I forged the key,
Unlocked the door...
At last, I am free;
My soul and body roar.

My girl conceived the plot,
She knew my pedigree;
We quickly tied the knot,
We longed for our glee.

Today, we are on cloud nine,
Today, we are forever free,
Our life is spotlessly divine,
Like Eden's Wisdom Tree.

We Never Kissed Goodbye

The melody of rain,
Echoes my mother's lullaby,
I can't escape my pain,
We never kissed goodbye.

Mom sang her songs
Almost an octave shy,
I did my rights and wrongs,
We never kissed goodbye.

I'll heal my scars and dents,
But how to forget until I die
Her smile, her tender hands;
We never kissed goodbye.

Somewhere amid the stars
I am sure she learned to fly,
I am still wasted in the bars;
We never kissed goodbye.

I lost; nothing is gained,
My hands are chained,
My soul is cold; I sinned,
The jury has been sworn,
They'll hang me up to dry,
I'll sway naked in the wind,
No one will cry and mourn,
We'll never kiss goodbye.

Dawn filled the world
With loud pleasing voices,
It was the last accord
Over cacophony of noises.
My troubled life passed by,
I heard my mother's sigh,
We'll never kiss goodbye.

We Saved Some Poppies

Across the fields of war,
Under our fallen bodies
We saved some poppies,
We died; we are no more.

Only the church's bell
Will sadly ring and tell
The truth about our wars,
About our final chores
On distant foreign shores,
About our endless fights,
About our sleepless nights,
About our weeping mothers
And our kids without fathers.

Saved poppies in the fight
Bloom as metamorphoses
Of our futile wars,
The orphans wake in fright,
And never see their fathers
At the doors.

My verses leave no traces,
I still enjoy my daily bread,
I quote my humble graces,
Those poppies are still red
In those abandoned places,
My nightmares wait in bed.

We Split the Hair

We split the hair
At times, it is unfair;
We are only fair
When we chew the air.

I want to wash the feet
Of those who knew defeat,
I want to turn the tables
Against the myths and fables.

The streams of rain
Run into the angry river,
The river roars in vain
As if she has a fever.

The sky is clearer
I swiftly readjust the sail;
We used to say,
My ducks are lined,
My train is on the rails;
The ripples run behind
In my old rearview mirror.

I was victorious in my last strife,
I tried to calm the river of my life,
I asked, to have or not to have,
To put these verses on the shelf
Or just to pour another glass?
I only heard: IN VINO VERITAS!

We Tried to Bathe our Souls

Don't clip our wings,
Don't gild our cage,
Three eastern kings
Will need the stage.

We take the bribes,
We lose our honors,
We dump our brides,
We mourn the goners.

Life moves as a polished carriage,
We cherish diamonds and gold
The cornerstones of any marriage,
We always bluff, we never fold.

We navigated stormy seas
Amid the wrecks and glitches,
We saw our shattered dreams;
We saw the wars without peace,
We saw the wounds and stitches,
We saw the bloodstained streams.

We tried to bathe our souls
In morning dew of our whims,
We climbed the to reach our goals
We touched our endurance rims.

We Tried to Love Somebody Else

We tried to love somebody else,
Someone besides ourselves,
As if we heard the church's bells
Inviting us upstairs.

We reaped what we have sowed,
We knew the cracks on every road,
On every avenue and street
That march to their own beat.

Easily forgiving duplicities of many,
But not a mere originality of one,
We wouldn't share even a penny
With those who're not like everyone.

We kill those whom we love,
Those who are strong, by swords,
Those who are weak, by kisses;
We choke them with an iron glove,
We mud them with the nasty words,
Yet praise self-admiration of Narcissus.

We listen to our friends and foes,
But hear the voices of ancestors
That tried to disconnect the dots.
We always stand upon our toes
To be above the common jesters,
Above the circles and the squares,
And walk across the broken pots
Of our well forgotten love affairs.

We Walk through Gauntlets

We walk through gauntlets,
Through corridors of powers,
Hallucinations daunt us
Until our final happy hours.

We are in a rusty cage of war,
The powerholders tightly lock it,
We fight; they keep the score;
They live; we kick the bucket.

I have returned from service,
Maples already shed their gold,
The trees are cold and nervous,
I am not nervous; I am cold.

My old retriever licks my cheeks,
My daughter doesn't know who I am,
My son is small and hardly speaks,
My wife excitedly destroyed the dam
And runs the river of her happy tears
Between our kisses, hugs and cheers.

I brought no presents
To my kids and wife,
Under the alien crescents
I gave away my soul for life.

Footprints of a vanished summer
Resting under the autumn leaves,
A rain is like a gloomy drummer
Plays requiem and deeply grieves.

We Went to See Magritte

Late golden Fall
Fell from above
On our first ever kiss,
On our first ever love;
She gave me all,
I soared to bliss.

I am an ordinary boy,
Naughty and merry,
I had a vicious ploy,
I craved her cherry.

We used my mother's car,
Parked right behind the bar;
First time for both,
Two loves; one troth.
We drank each other's scent,
Young eager animals in heat,
The angels envied our ascent
Above the squeaky seat...

And then...Renee Magritte:
Nostalgic crescents in the sky,
The trees are strangely lit,
Umbrellas hang or numbly fly.

Insanity of nights,
Tranquility of days,
A rather perfect science:
No wrongs, no rights,
No predators, no preys,
A quiet glory of defiance.

We went to see Magritte,
First time for all. That's it.

Where Am I From?

They always ask
Where I am from,
It's not an easy task:
I am sorry, I forgot,
I never had a home,
It was a parking lot.

There is no smoke,
Unless there is a fire,
I've been forever broke,
My past was rather dire.

My hours have passed,
I run beyond the bounds,
The demons of the past,
Those merciless hounds
Will never die; they last,
They make their rounds.

Where am I from?
I know where I dwell,
The heaven is my home,
Meanwhile my life is hell.

White Lilacs Gently Gleam

I turn the wheel,
Worn tires squeal,
They hardly handle
The walks of lives;
I strike the pedal,
The highway flies.

Protected by the nasty guards
An angel deals a deck of cards
To greedy predators and prey.
Is it the final judgement day?

I see descending love,
And walk under its rays,
I crave a second dove
To share my happy days.

Our orbits never crossed
Above the sparkling dew,
Invite me, be my host,
Life is a pas de deux.

The witnesses of our youth,
Old lilacs sway their twigs,
A lovely scent will soothe
The pain of broken wings.

Life made a great bouquet,
White lilacs gently gleam,
Don't throw them away,
Don't kill my fragile dream.

Wisdom is Always Blind

Wisdom is always blind,
Like a sclerotic maven:
A harbor for my mind,
A hidden, quiet haven,
A playfield for the wild,
An intellectual lovechild.

Surprising rite of spring
Awakened curly streams,
The birds relearned to fly.
An old swan starts to sing,
It is farewell, it is goodbye,
I cry and kiss my dreams.

Although the clouds hover
And disobey their master
Like servants at the end.
I lost my future as a lover,
But gained a loyal friend,
In spite of this disaster.

Somebody conjures up
A perfectly untouched daydream,
The muddled shapes of which
Dissolve and blur before my eyes;
It was my angel's morbid scheme,
His hand already tossed the dice.

My wisdom hasn't gone
It reached the fertile sun.

Without Our Sins

I am an anxious mess,
It is a merciless winter;
Scotch lulls my stress
In a warmed-up snifter.

The light still streams,
Manipulates my hopes,
Then whips my dreams
And yanks the ropes.

It is the winter's farewell plot,
It is the winter's parting blow,
The miserable crunchy snow
Falls on the empty parking lot.

Two swirling brittle snowflakes,
The innocent and gentle twins
Without our horrible mistakes,
Without our inevitable sins,
Died in my trembling hands
Like two inseparable friends.

I am floating downstream
Like an abandoned pup
Toward a stepping stone.
Don't interrupt my dream,
Don't try to wake me up,
Please, let me be alone.

The fiery Elijah's ride
Still lingering inside
Of every day I lived,
Of every blessing I received.
I dream of castles in the sky,
I close my eyes. Goodbye.

Without Peace in Sight

I looked far back
And knew full well,
If I'll run my track,
I'll finish up in hell.

I walked along two hostile worlds,
Abandoned by two fighting hordes,
A narrow path between two goals,
Amid the graveyards for the souls,
Without days, without nights,
But flanked by blinding lights.

No dusks, no dawns,
No stars, no clouds,
Above the fallen pawns,
Above the bloody grounds.

Life has to lock the doors
Before we're shoved inside
Into the never-ending wars
Without a peace in sight.

Wrapped in My Art

New Christmas trees
Determinedly grow
Down from the skies;
Before a pastel dawn
I pulled a lovely one
With silver filigrees.

A fiery sunset's glow
Brings cracking ashes
Out of watersplashes,
Out of long goodbyes.

Only the ancient vines
Yield tasty morsels;
And interlace the lines
To shape my verses.

I made our town mad,
The time stood still,
You sensed a déjà vu,
You were too sad,
I didn't go downhill,
I paddled our canoe.

At dawn, I willingly
Laid bare my heart,
I brought you glee
Wrapped in my art.

You Hold a Password to My Heart

The sun is carefully rising,
There is a sail on the horizon,
It is my aimless, lonely soul
In the pursuit of the Black hole.

The ripples sway white lace,
My boat enjoys a slow pace,
It moves like a sleepy swan,
It glides in the beams of sun.

You hold a password to my heart,
You wish I will give away my art
To my mean critics' legal papers
To septic whispers of the waiters,
To dreary mornings
And chilly breezing,
To useless warnings
About the abyss that's freezing.

Don't use a password to my heart,
Don't put a dam across the stream,
Be wary, don't aim at me your dart,
Don't kill the innocence of our dream.

Youth Was a One-Night Stand

Youth was just a one-night stand.
I meandered from the primal day
In labyrinths of yet unknown land,
While years painted my hair gray.

The powerholders of those days
Marched in their muddy boots
Through my integrity and grace
Straight to my yet fragile roots.

My destiny was built on sand,
I walked and ran on feet of clay,
My victories were seldom planned.
I only scored my failures every day.

Please, hear my anxious groans
And comprehend their meaning,
Milestones became tombstones
While red sunsets were gleaming.

My hopes ascended into bliss,
Returned as flowers of spring,
As innocence of a baby's kiss,
As tunes the birds forever sing.

At night, when the darkness falls
My memories cast shadows
On the walls,
And only my ever-trembling hand
Reminds me that my youth
Was just a one-night stand.

Epilogue

The Poet lights the light and fades away...
But the light goes on and on.

Emily Dickinson

Acknowledgments

I am deeply and endlessly grateful to Judith Broadbent for her skilled professional guldens and generous stewardship; for her unyielding yet wise editing which gave me enough room to exercise my whims.

To Anna Dikalova for her kind ideas and a firm belief In my success.

To a great artist, Mary Anne Capeci, who allowed me to use her painting for the cover of this book.

To all my friends for their continuous and gently Expressed motivations.

Thanks, y'all.

Printed in the United States
by Baker & Taylor Publisher Services